CW00537350

THE VICTORIA AND ALBERT COLOUR BOOKS

FIRST PUBLISHED IN GREAT BRITAIN BY
WEBB & BOWER (PUBLISHERS) LIMITED
9 COLLETON CRESCENT, EXETER, DEVON EX2 4 BY
AND MICHAEL JOSEPH LIMITED, 27 WRIGHTS LANE, LONDON W8 5TZ
IN ASSOCIATION WITH THE VICTORIA AND ALBERT MUSEUM, LONDON



FIRST PUBLISHED 1987
SECOND IMPRESSION MAY 1987
THIRD IMPRESSION AUGUST 1987
FOURTH IMPRESSION MARCH 1988

BOOK, COVER AND SLIP CASE DESIGN BY CARROLL, DEMPSEY & THIRKELL LIMITED

BRITISH LIBRARY CATALOGUING IN PUBLICATION DATA

YOUNG, HILARY
FLORAL BORDERS-(THE VICTORIA AND ALBERT COLOUR BOOKS)
1. BORDERS, ORNAMENTAL (DECORATIVE ARTS)
2. DECORATION AND ORNAMENT-PLANT FORMS
1. TITLE II. SERIES
745.4 NK3630.4.B67

ISBN 0-86350-149-4



PRODUCTION BY FACER PUBLISHING
COLOUR REPRODUCTION BY PENINSULAR REPRO SERVICE, EXETER
TYPESET IN GREAT BRITAIN BY OPTIC

PRINTED AND BOUND IN HONG KONG BY
MANDARIN OFFSET

THE VICTORIA AND ALBERT COLOUR BOOKS

# FLORAL BORDERS

INTRODUCTION BY
HILARY YOUNG

WEBB & BOWER
MICHAEL JOSEPH
MCMLXXXVII

THE BORDERS reproduced in this book have been selected from three albums, purchased by the Victoria and Albert Museum in 1986, which contain nearly 800 patterns and original designs for printed cottons. The contents of these albums range in date from the last quarter of the eighteenth century to the middle of the nineteenth century, with the years 1790 to 1810 – often considered a golden age for printed tex tiles – being particularly well represented. Since Continental material of this date and of such remarkably high quality has not previously been well represented at the Museum, the albums constitute one of the most important additions to the collection of textile designs made in recent years.

Among the designs are many that are inscribed in French with technical notes and instructions to the cutters of the printing blocks. Other designs bear notes in German, and three are inscribed in Italian; none, unfortunately, is dated. It has not been possible to attribute the designs to a specific printworks, but it seems likely that they were intended for production either at Mulhouse, a town now in France and situated near the border with Germany, or somewhat further north in the area that is now the French Haut Rhin *département* of Upper Alsace.

Much has been discovered by the curators of the Musée de l'Impression sur Etoffes de Mulhouse about the founding and development of the textile trades at Mulhouse and Alsace (see Bibliography). The firm of Koechlin,

Schmaltzer et Cie was founded in 1747 and was the first of a large number of partnerships, many of whom were connected with one another, to print cottons at Mulhouse. Production spread to nearby towns on the Upper Rhine, notably to Logelbach, Colmar and Wesserling; none of these however rivalled the output of Mulhouse. The products of the workshops of these towns were often closely related in style – possibly they employed the same designers – and it is by comparison with documented textiles and designs preserved at Mulhouse that the attribution of the contents of the albums to this area of eastern France has been made.

The albums contain both original designs in pen, watercolour and body-colour and impressions taken from the woodblocks and engraved copper-plates used to print the fabric, some of which have additional colouring by hand. The printed impressions, which are known as patterns (used here with the supplementary meaning of an 'example' or 'specimen'), were made as factory records or in order to show to prospective clients. Many of the designs are numbered, but the numbering does not follow a continuous chronological sequence – indeed, one design has a border numbered 2839 and a filling pattern inscribed *'intérieur No. 3691'* – and it seems likely that at least two, and probably more, numerical sequences were used. Within the albums the designs do not follow these numbers, rather their compiler seems to have made an attempt to group similar types of pattern together. For example, all the designs for mourning chintz are pasted in at the end of one album, as are those for 'Cashmere' patterns. Consequently, designs that differ widely in date have in many cases been pasted on to the same page. The albums and the portfolios that enclose them date from the late nineteenth century and their contents probably formed part of an archive of patterns and designs from one or more printworks.

The border patterns were intended to be reproduced by means of wooden printing blocks. They were used for handkerchiefs, tablecloths and shawls, and also for curtains and other furnishing fabrics. Among the earliest examples in the collection is a group of seven original designs by an unidentified artist; these date from about 1790, certainly no later, and are

represented here by two examples *(plates 1 and 2)*. Typically these are of doves among fruit and flowers, or of birds clambering over medallions of classical ruins or pastoral scenes. Compared with the designs of about five to ten years later the ornament is here sparsely deployed, for during the later 1790s designers were seeking far bolder effects. To this end clear geometrical structures were made use of. Quadrant shapes, for example, were sometimes introduced at the corners, and the floral trails were often bounded on both sides by bands of abstract neo-classical ornament *(plate 30, below)*. Where the direction of the pattern changed at the corners, this was often emphasized by breaking the floral repeat and introducing squares enclosing circular medallions *(plates 3 and 4)*.

These changes in composition were accompanied with and complemented by a change in the type of floral ornament employed. The scale of the flowers was increased, and the flowers themselves were in many instances depicted with painstaking attention to botanical accuracy *(plates 4 and 5)*. Frequently the main pattern was set over a sub-pattern of mossy trails on a dark ground, the fashion for which was most marked during the 1790s *(plates 9-11)*.

Many of the designs of the 1790s combine extraordinary richness of detail with great vibrancy of colour. For the realization of these effects the designers were dependent upon the high standard that had been attained in cutting wooden printing blocks – into which copper wires were sometimes embedded – and on the progress that had been made in the understanding of the properties of dyes, thickeners and mordants. That the print-block cutters, at least, were equal to this task is clearly demonstrated by a number of

block impressions from the albums *(plates 3, 5, 14, 16, 19)*.

The last impression, plate 14, is reproduced opposite an original design with a similar pattern of poppies; so close are the two that they must have been designed by the same hand. Among the designs and impressions are several others that can be grouped according to their authorship. For example, the floral border in plate 3 can be securely attributed to the artist who drew the designs in the facing illustration; in fact, all the elements on the central border of the latter are to be found in the impression on plate 3, though they are arranged slightly differently. Plates 25 and 26 are by the same hand, as are 27 and 28. Similarly, plates 9, 10 and 11 can be attributed to one hand.

Plate 9 is of considerable interest since it is almost identical to, and clearly by the same artist as, a drawing in the Cooper-Hewitt Museum, New York. The New York drawing is one of a group of designs signed by Louis-Albert Du Bois (1752-1818), an artist who is known to have provided designs between about 1780 and 1800 for the Fabrique de Fazy aux Bergues, Geneva. The Victoria and Albert Museum's albums also contain designs, not reproduced here, that are identical in style to examples in the Musée at Mulhouse. These examples are associated with the major textile centre of Jouy in France. The presence of these Jouy patterns and the designs by Du Bois among others attributable to Mulhouse and Alsace raises a number of intriguing questions. At least one manufacturer of printed scarves and handkerchiefs, Jean-Jacques Zurcher-Lischy of Mulhouse, is known to have been employed at the workshops of Fazy in Geneva before about 1785, and others may have had connections with this printworks. Special mention should be made of the design in plate 24. This is a representative example from a group of eight drawings by the same hand, some of which are inscribed in Italian. Its designer, like Du Bois, was perhaps from the Swiss Confederation of States (to which Mulhouse was allied until 1789). The design, with its corner motif of an amaryllus, illustrates one of the fashions of the years around 1800; similar exotic plant forms, but in this instance probably wholly the creation of the designer's imagination, can be seen in the facing illustration.

By the early 1800s designers had largely abandoned the elaborate, wide, neo-classical borders used on shawls and kerchiefs of the 1790s. The succeeding style, of floral trails on a white ground, is well represented in the collection. Several of these designs are drawn with a calligraphic freedom that suggests the influence of far-eastern painted silks *(plates 27-29)*. Others, of delicately drawn trails of strawberry plants or roses, appear to have been based on botanical studies *(plates 25 and 26)*; similar designs at Mulhouse are associated with the local firm of Risler and Koechlin. The related design in plate 30 is very close to others at Mulhouse which are dated 1801 and 1802 and which are attributed to Alsace.

Though the albums are rich in designs of the 1820s, especially those for dress-fabrics, they contain surprisingly little material that can be firmly dated to the previous decade. Designs for borders, representative of the late 1810s and 1820s, are reproduced in plate 18 (top left and bottom right) and plate 31. These were intended to be printed using a limited palette of only two or three colours and are of small abstract motifs or stylized floral forms. It is evident that a withdrawal from bold experimentation and the pursuit of naturalism had by then taken place. These are among the latest designs for borders in the collection. However, the albums also include many designs for printed dress-fabrics that date from as late as the middle of the nineteenth century. These repeating patterns – some of which were intended to be enclosed by borders of the type reproduced here – are the subject of *Patterns for Textiles*, a companion book in this series.

## BIBLIOGRAPHY

Albrecht-Mathey, E, *The Fabrics of Mulhouse and Alsace, 1750-1800*, Leigh-on-Sea, 1968.

Thomé Jacqué, J, *Chefs d'œuvre du Musée de l'Impression sur Etoffes, Mulhouse*, three volumes, Tokyo, 1978.

Tuchscherer, J M, *The Fabrics of Mulhouse and Alsace, 1801-1850*, Leigh-on-Sea, 1972.

Victoria and Albert Museum, *An American Museum of Decorative Art and Design: Designs from the Cooper-Hewitt Collection, New York*, London, 1973, Nos. 161-4.

Much help was given in the preparation of this book by Miss Natalie Rothstein.

## KEY TO PLATES

All works illustrated are in watercolour and/or bodycolour unless otherwise stated. Many of the impressions from woodblocks have additional colouring by hand.

*1-2.* c.1790, both by the same hand. *3.* border of sphinxes 1790s; polychrome floral border 1790s (impression from woodblocks, designed by the same hand as the borders in pl.4.). *4.* 1790s. *5.* top c.1790-5; bottom 1790s (impression from woodblocks). *6.* 1790s. *7-8.* c.1790-1800. *9-11.* c.1790-1800, borders by L-A Du Bois. *12.* top c.1800; left c.1795-1800; border 1790s. *13.* border of strawberries c.1800-5; border of poppies c.1790-1800. *14.* c.1790-1800 (impression from woodblocks, designed by the same hand as facing illustration of poppies). *15.* top left and bottom right c.1790-1800 (impressions from woodblocks); top right and bottom left c.1815-20. *16.* c.1790-1800 (impression from woodblocks). *17.* c.1795-1800. *18.* top left and bottom right c.1815-20; top right and bottom left c.1795-1800. *19.* top left 1790s; bottom c.1790-1800 (impression from woodblocks). *20.* c.1800. *21-22.* c.1795-1800; bottom right c.1800 (impressions from woodblocks, designed by the same hand). *23.* c.1800 (impression from woodblocks). *24.* c.1795-1800. *25-26.* c.1800-5, both designs by the same hand. *27-28.* c.1800-5, the two large floral borders by the same hand. *29.* floral border c.1800-5; narrow borders c.1790-1800. *30.* floral border c.1800-5; neo-classical border c.1800. *31.* top left and bottom right c.1795-1800; top right and bottom left c.1820-30. *32.* border c.1825; striped designs c.1790-1800.

THE PLATES

1

3

7

9

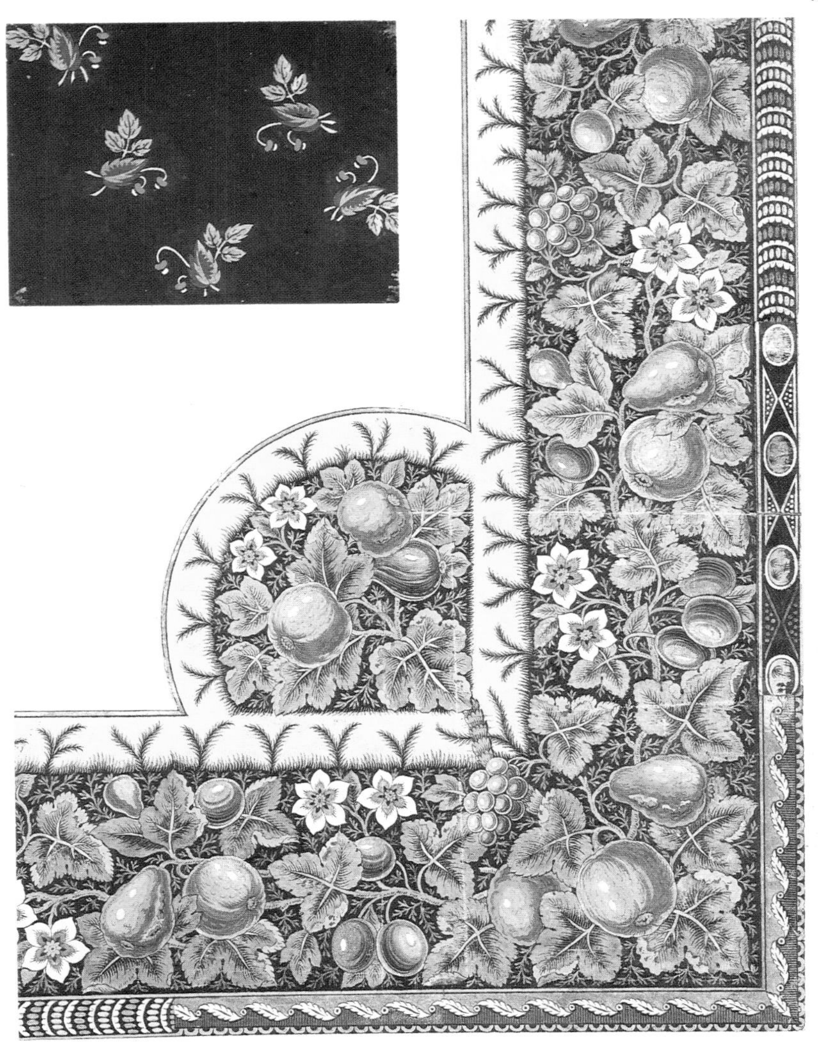

11

12

13

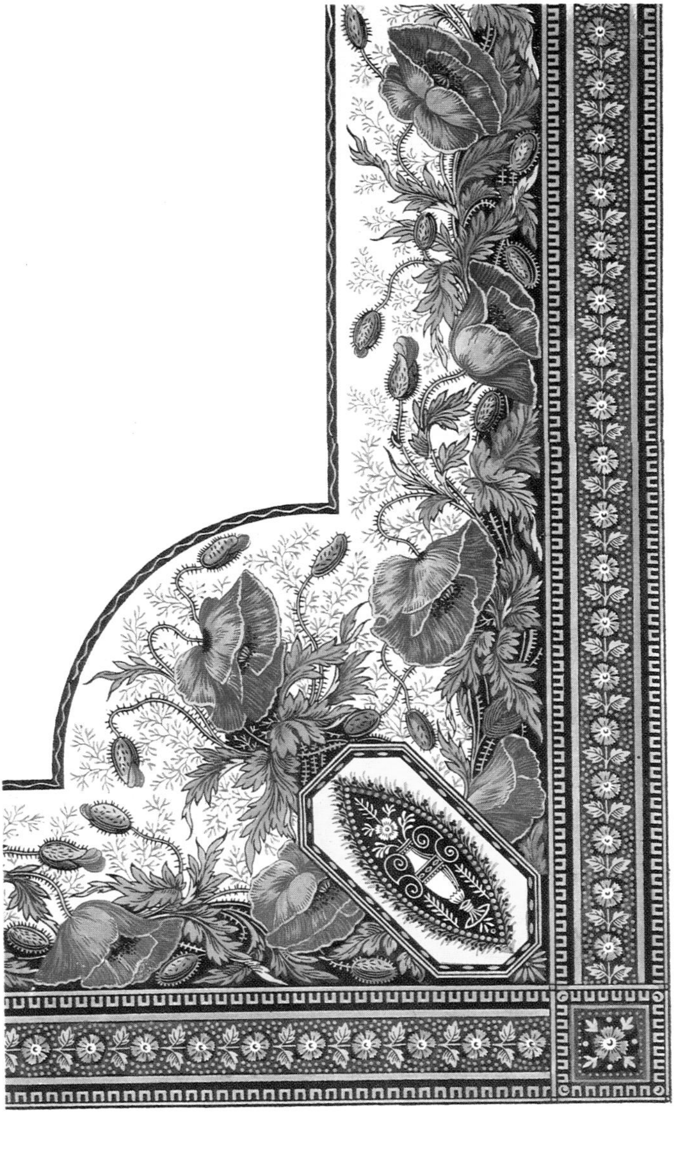

15

19

21

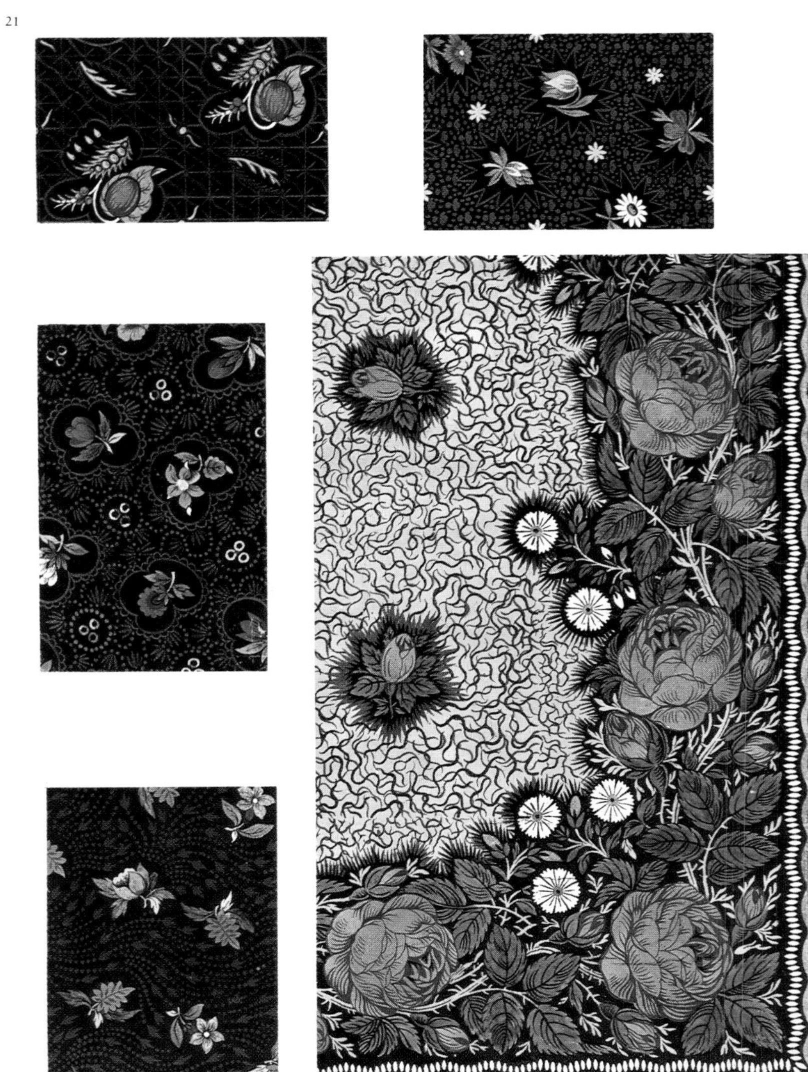

23

25

27

29